HOW IT WORKS
TELEVISIONS

by Rachel Hamby

FOCUS
READERS

WWW.FOCUSREADERS.COM

Focus Readers is distributed by North Star Editions:
sales@northstareditions.com | 888-417-0195

Produced for Focus Readers by Red Line Editorial.

Content Consultant: Robert J. Thompson, Director, Bleier Center for Television and Popular Culture, Syracuse University

Photographs ©: Andrey Popov/iStockphoto, cover, 1; bonetta/iStockphoto, 4–5; Ann Ronan Picture Library Heritage Images/Newscom, 7; Red Line Editorial, 8; IxMaster/Shutterstock Images, 10–11; monkeybusinessimages/iStockphoto, 13; Sean Pavone/Shutterstock Images, 15; Vertigo3d/iStockphoto, 16–17; jakkapan21/iStockphoto, 19; marcociannarel/iStockphoto, 21; scyther5/iStockphoto, 22–23; ttsz/iStockphoto, 25; Sorbis/Shutterstock Images, 26–27; sdominick/iStockphoto, 29

ISBN
978-1-63517-237-9 (hardcover)
978-1-63517-302-4 (paperback)
978-1-63517-432-8 (ebook pdf)
978-1-63517-367-3 (hosted ebook)

Library of Congress Control Number: 2017935886

Printed in the United States of America
Mankato, MN
June, 2017

ABOUT THE AUTHOR

Rachel Hamby was born in Utah, the same state where the inventor of the electronic television was born. Now she lives in Spokane, Washington, where she watches television with her husband and a corgi that loves nature programs. She also writes poems and stories for kids.

TABLE OF CONTENTS

CHAPTER 1

INSPIRATION AND INVENTION

Every day, millions of people pick up their remotes and watch their favorite shows. But few understand the science taking place behind the screen.

A TV is actually part of a system that sends and receives video and audio information. First, the information is broken down into electronic signals.

For a TV set to work, it must receive sound and picture information.

Then the signals are sent out. Finally, a **receiver** picks up the signals and turns them back into sound and images.

Inventors of the TV were inspired by radio technology. Because sound could be transmitted over the air without wires, they wondered if pictures could be transmitted, too. John Logie Baird built the first TV system in 1926. It used two spinning discs. Glass lenses around the first disc picked up light from the object. The light hit a **photoelectric cell**. This cell changed the light energy into electric signals.

The signals were sent by wire to a receiver. The receiver used a second

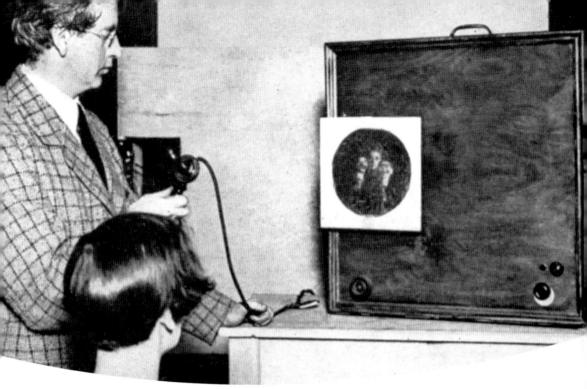

The first TV images were not very clear and often flickered.

spinning disc to create an image of the object. It used a process called scanning. Starting at one corner, the disc created one line of the image at a time.

Philo T. Farnsworth made the first electronic TV in 1927. His TV system used cathode rays instead of spinning discs.

A cathode ray is a beam of **electrons** that is made inside a vacuum tube. The electronic TV system had one cathode ray tube in the camera. Another tube was in the receiver. To make an image, a cathode ray in the camera picked up light from the object. Then a cathode ray in the receiver reassembled the image. The ray hit a glass screen at the end of the tube.

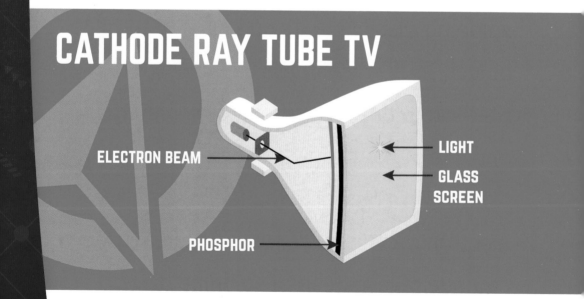

CATHODE RAY TUBE TV

ELECTRON BEAM

LIGHT

GLASS SCREEN

PHOSPHOR

The screen was coated in phosphor. The phosphor made the screen light up when it was hit by the ray. The ray scanned one row of the image at a time.

For several years, TVs only displayed black-and-white images. In the 1950s, inventors made a system to broadcast colors, too. Color TVs used three electron beams. One beam was red. One was green. The third was blue. Together, the beams scanned an image onto the screen. The three colors blended together. This made a full range of colors in the image.

By 1972, more color TVs were sold than black-and-white TVs. Since then, TVs have continued to improve.

CHAPTER 2

SENDING SIGNALS

Sound and picture information is sent to a TV as a signal. To create signals, cameras and microphones capture light and sound. At first, TVs used **analog** signals. A camera split each image into a series of electrical impulses. The impulses created a signal, which varied depending on how bright the light was.

Places where TV cameras record programming are called studios.

Dark areas of the image made weak electrical impulses. Bright areas made strong impulses.

Microphones picked up sound to go with the images. They changed the sound into electrical impulses, too. These impulses created a signal that varied depending on the sound's pitch.

TV stations broadcast these signals. An antenna on the station's transmission tower sent the signals out on radio waves. The radio waves traveled through the air. Antennas on viewers' roofs picked up the radio waves. Then the antennas sent the radio waves to the viewers' TVs.

With just a TV receiver and antenna, viewers can watch programs on many channels for free.

In 2009, US broadcasts switched to digital signals. This method encodes the image and sound into **bits**. Each bit represents a small part of the image or sound. Like analog signals, digital signals are sent out over radio waves.

However, digital signals can carry more information over longer distances. They provide clearer pictures and sound, too.

Signals can also be sent through cords or cables. Cable TV companies use coaxial cables to bring signals to people's homes. Devices such as DVD players might use other cables, such as HDMI cables. These connect into ports on the back of the TV. This brings the signal from the device to the TV.

Some TVs get signals from satellites. A dish on or near the viewer's home picks up the signals. Cables then carry the signals from the dish to the TV. Other TVs

Satellite dishes are often placed on roofs.

can **stream** signals by connecting to the Internet.

Viewers select different options on the TV's menu. This allows them to switch between a broadcast, a streamed Internet program, or another device.

CHAPTER 3

TUNING IN

A TV receives signals and changes them back into light and sound. Each TV channel has a specific **frequency**. The **tuner** finds the radio wave that matches the selected channel. Then, the tuner removes the digital audio and video signals from the radio wave.

A tuner can pick up many different kinds of programs.

These signals are still encoded. The tuner decodes the signals. The signals are turned back into electrical charges.

Next, the tuner sends the video signals to the video circuit board. From there, the signals are sent to the screen, where the electrical energy is turned back into light. The tuner sends the audio signals to the audio circuit board. This circuit board sends the signals to the speakers. The speakers turn the signals back into sound.

CRITICAL THINKING

Why do the digital signals need to be decoded before they are sent to the video and audio circuit boards?

A circuit board contains many small electronic parts.

The tuner also syncs the video and audio information. This makes the pictures and sound play together. Finally, the tuner formats the video to fit the size of the TV screen.

REMOTE CONTROL

A remote control sends coded signals to a TV. The signals can perform actions such as changing the channel, controlling the sound, and turning the TV on or off. Inside a remote control is a circuit board. The circuit board is a thin piece of fiberglass with copper wires etched onto the surface. For each button on the remote, there is a disk on the circuit board. This disk can conduct electricity.

When a person presses the remote's button, a connection is made between the button and the disk. This connection sends an electrical charge. The charge travels down a copper wire to an electronic circuit called a chip. The chip produces a code specific to that button. It sends the code to an infrared light-emitting diode (LED). The

A remote control also allows viewers to access the TV's menu.

infrared signal is sent to the TV. It tells the TV which function to perform.

CHAPTER 4

BEHIND THE SCREEN

The images on a TV screen appear to be moving. But they are actually a series of individual images. Each image is slightly different. By displaying the images very quickly, a TV tricks viewers' eyes into seeing a moving picture.

Flat-screen TVs use small dots known as pixels to create each image.

Some LCD TVs can display more than 16 million colors.

Each image is made up of many rows of pixels. Each pixel contains three subpixels. One is red. One is green. The third is blue. Together, they can create a wide variety of colors.

In liquid crystal display (LCD) TVs, liquid crystals are arranged in a grid of columns and rows. The crystals are between layers of electrodes. Two polarizing filters control the type of light waves that pass through. The filters cause the light waves to follow a specific pattern.

To light up a particular pixel, the electrodes send a charge down a column and a row. The charge travels through the liquid crystals. It causes the crystals to twist. This allows light to pass through a pixel and the filter. Changing the charge's strength controls how bright the light is.

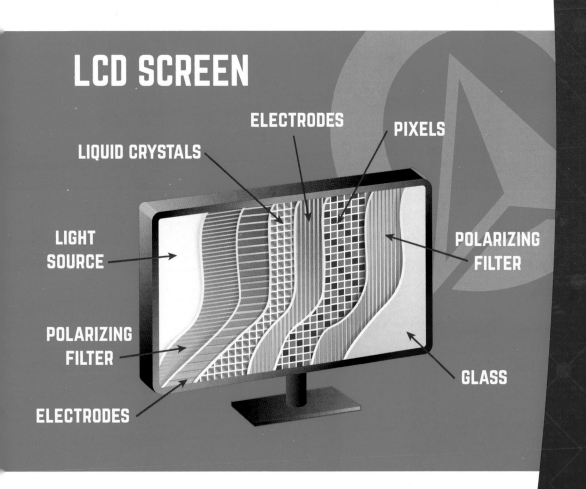

LCD SCREEN

ELECTRODES

PIXELS

LIQUID CRYSTALS

LIGHT SOURCE

POLARIZING FILTER

POLARIZING FILTER

ELECTRODES

GLASS

Panasonic
LED
SAMSUNG
UA65H7500
3D LED SMART TV
$29980
$23880
LG ULTRA H
4K
SONY
FIFA TV
X8500B
ent of soccer
Foot
HIGHLIGHT PLAYER
00:05:00
WATCH
HIGHLIGHTS
WATCH
THE LATEST
CLIPS
13.11.25 | 00:18:00
13.11.25 | 00:24:00

CHAPTER 5

IMPROVING QUALITY

High-definition TVs (HDTVs) were introduced in the late 1990s. Their wide displays imitated the screens used in movie theaters. This new shape allowed HDTVs to show a wider angle of an image. HDTVs also had more pixels in their screens. As a result, they could display clearer, more detailed pictures.

Ultra-HDTV screens can have more than 8 million pixels.

Today, Ultra-HDTVs use even more pixels. They display even higher-quality images.

Showing more images per second helps TVs imitate lifelike movement. Older TVs display 25 to 30 images each second. But newer TVs can display up to 120 images per second.

A smart TV combines a TV set with a computer. Viewers connect smart TVs to the Internet. Then, they can stream programs, play games, use apps, and much more.

CRITICAL THINKING

Why would it be helpful that HDTVs can show wider angles of images?

Smart TVs can even connect to users' smartphones.

Companies can also make 3D TVs. These TVs display two images at once. Viewers wear special glasses. The glasses cause each eye to see a slightly different image. This makes the images seem to have depth. Some companies are working to make 3D TVs that work without glasses. They are known as Ultra-D TVs. People continue designing TVs to display sharper, clearer pictures.

FOCUS ON
TELEVISIONS

Write your answers on a separate piece of paper.

1. Write a sentence that explains the main idea of Chapter 2.

2. Would you rather have a 3D TV or a smart TV? Why?

3. What part decodes the signals into information a TV can display?

    A. the antenna
    B. the speaker
    C. the tuner

4. What would happen if the electrodes in a TV screen did not send an electrical charge through the liquid crystals?

    A. Sound would not come out of the speakers.
    B. Light would not go through the pixels.
    C. Signals would not be received by the antenna.

Answer key on page 32.

GLOSSARY

analog
Measuring or representing data by using a continuously changing signal instead of by using numbers.

bits
Units of information in computing and digital communication. Each bit has a value of zero or one.

electrons
Charged particles that can be in atoms or on their own.

frequency
The number of cycles per second that a radio wave has.

photoelectric cell
A device that generates an electric current whose strength depends on the brightness of the light hitting it.

receiver
A device that picks up and converts radio waves or other signals.

stream
To send or receive a steady flow of data.

tuner
The part of a TV that converts radio waves back to audio and video signals.

TO LEARN MORE

BOOKS

Laine, Carolee. *Inventing the Television*. Mankato, MN: The Child's World, 2016.

Otfinoski, Steven. *Television: From Concept to Consumer*. New York: Children's Press, 2015.

Spilsbury, Richard, and Louise Spilsbury. *The Television*. Chicago: Heinemann Library, 2012.

NOTE TO EDUCATORS

Visit **www.focusreaders.com** to find lesson plans, activities, links, and other resources related to this title.

INDEX

Answer Key: 1. Answers will vary; 2. Answers will vary; 3. C; 4. B